OLD BEDFO

For My Father who Grew Up in Old Bedfordshire

Published 1975

ISBN 0 900804 15 7

Printed and published by

WHITE CRESCENT PRESS LTD, LUTON

OLD BEDFORDSHIRE

A Collection of 145 Old Photographs

SIMON HOUFE

INDEX

Index (continued)

CONTENTS

A Victorian Lens

The photographs in this book are an attempt to gather together pictures of the Bedfordshire of the day before yesterday. Although the selection is subject to my own preferences and tastes, the pictures seem to have logically grouped themselves into those years when the county was still predominantly rural and industry and change were curiosities. One of these changes was the development of the camera itself and it arrived sufficiently early on the scene to capture a legacy of unspoiled, unindustrialised, uncluttered landscape. The earliest prints appear to date from the 1850s when the dominance of the mailcoach, the Repeal of the Corn Laws and even the Battle of Waterloo were clearly remembered. The latest are in the 1930s when factories, airfields and ribbon development were already chewing into the contours of a very small county. Perhaps the vanishing point of this world was the 1930s or the mid-1940s when I can vividly remember the teams of cart-horses plodding to the fields through a sleeping Ampthill at five in the morning. A vanishing point must exist if the photographs here seem to give a composite picture of their own period and yet are so different from our own; at some particular moment the shutter must have closed for the last time on a way of life.

For me, that time comes with the close of the village as a self-sufficient community, its own hub of news, gossip, lore and culture, a web of houses linked to school, church and chapel. It was still possible in 1930 to be very isolated in a Bedfordshire village, trips to the county town were planned weeks in advance, trips to London were a dream. Drainage, medical attention, social services and communications were in their infancy, but were compensated for by a greater sense of belonging and rich local traditions.

As these pages reveal, the needs of most villagers were supplied by their neighbours. The ironwork, hooks, bolts, bits and bridles, twine, sacking and implements, today searched for in vain in a dozen supermarkets, were made on their doorstep. They would quite rightly regard our carting of produce backwards and forwards across the country as ridiculous, our reliance on milk, not from the stomach of a cow but from the three-day-old pasteurised stomach of a tanker lorry as both contemptible and derisory. For the blacksmith and the wheelwright there was excellence of work not cost effectiveness, for the carrier and the mason, demand not viability, waste and built-in obsolesence were beyond the average person's comprehension. If our Victorian lens appears to be growing rose-tinted, it is tempting to ask which is a richer inheritance, a county of words where every village had its own flower and insect names or a county of no words, but open mouths in front of the television?

It was the wealth of language, dialect and legend that Dean Burgon recognised in his walks through the lanes of Houghton Conquest in the 1870s. It was the same earthy philosophy that Arnold Bennett admired in Hockliffe in the 1900s. The camera came to focus its relentless lens on the people that gave all this vibrant life, the itinerants, carriers, bakers, cobblers and postmen. It recorded their dress, their mannerisms, their recreations, spying for us in every detail of their cottages and shops.

Country house life was likewise very much an integral part of the landscape of the village. Only the smallest hamlets were without a large farmhouse or manor, many villages were ringed by estates. Even in the age of photography, a majority of the villagers were either tenants, agricultural labourers, keepers, servants or traders with these establishments. Their households were vast, but so was the amount of entertaining undertaken as can be seen here at Ampthill House and Woburn Abbey. Through the private albums of these families one can glimpse card parties and groups in crowded interiors and catch sight through the open windows of perfect gardens tended by a numerous staff.

The camera was not only a recorder or a mode of business, it was a diversion. Between 1862 and 1877 photographers burgeon in most of the county's towns in answer to a growing demand. In 1862 the *Bedford Almanack* lists one photographer, by 1877 there are five in the county town, two at Luton and one each at Dunstable, Woburn, Biggleswade and Leighton Buzzard. Ten years later it is sixteen and by 1906 thirty. Even the earliest photographer to advertise, John G. Nall of Bedford recognised the appeal of the countryside. In 1862 he announced the sale of 'Photographic Portraits of Local Interest' and included local celebrities and village churches. Downes of Bedford advertised 'Objects of Interest in the County' in 1886 and Bindon of Luton specialised in 'portrait, architectural and landscape' photography. Frederick Thurston of Luton who produced the finest negatives of the period, advertised with justification his 'art in photography'. By the mid-1880s the householder could also enjoy stereoscopic views of local beauty spots like Houghton House and Flitton Mausoleum in 3-D at his own fireside! Views were produced in *carte-de-visite* size, too small to appreciate detail or as large as T. B. Latchmore's Houghton shown here, 7½ inches by 9½ inches. It is difficult to be sure what proportion of the work here is professional and what amateur. The latter were well catered for with apparatus shops in 1900, but strangely only one man in this collection has left exact details of his work (Plate 87).

The Victorian photographer appreciated the use of his camera for leisure and the recording of scenes and portraits, but not action. It will be noticed that the earlier photographers pose workmen in groups, as at Elstow, (Plate 114) or as portraits as with the gamekeeper (Plate 18) but never working. It was not simply long exposure but an attitude of mind. It was left to the Edwardians to discover the working photograph and more importantly the idea of *reportage*. The Victorian recorded events like the laying of a foundation stone (Plate 126) but the Edwardians began to see a car accident (Plate 132) or a train crash as news. If the Edwardians began to grasp the newsworthy value of the camera, they also began to use its more sentimental side. It is open to question how accurate a view of country life we get from the picture of straw-plaiting at Barton (Plate 39) where costume and figures seem to be arranged. A closer glimpse of a family in their working clothes in the south of the county is probably obtained in the Gravenhurst family (Plate 28).

Lastly I must make apologies to those whose villages are not included, I have tried to cast as wide a net as possible, but often no suitable prints exist or I do not know of them.

S. R. Houfe
Avenue House
AMPTHILL

The Beginnings of Photography

1. An old house at Ravensden from a photograph taken in the 1850s. Even at this early date the possibilities of recording buildings and landscape was being realised.

2. The Old Oak in Ampthill Park, about 1855. From the album of the Thynne family of Hawnes Park, Haynes.

3. Houghton House, Ampthill, about 1860. The ruins of this transitional mansion of 1615 were a favourite picnic spot for the Victorians, its decay was rapid between this date and 1900.

4. The 14th Lord St John and his family on the steps of Melchbourne Park, about 1862. Day dresses for the ladies and almost timeless country clothes for the men.

The Village

5. *High Street, Turvey, about 1900.*

6. *Silsoe village, about 1910. The 'George' Hotel on the left, then in the proprietorship of John Palmer Gray. The weather-boarded house is unusual even on the east side of the county.*

7. Looking towards All Saints church, Turvey, about 1900. The village street was a natural playground and many traditional games originated there.

8. Old cottages near the church at Stagsden, about 1900.

9. Church Road, Flitwick, about 1900. View looking towards the 'Fir Tree' public house, the sixteenth century cottage on the right survives but the thatched pair and the barn on the left have vanished.

10. Thatched cottages and village postman at Gravenhurst, about 1910.

11. The Moot Hall, Elstow, about 1880. This shows the building before its restoration with the doors and windows of the lower floor still bricked up.

12. The Manor House: Turvey Abbey photographed in about 1880 during the ownership of Charles Longuet Higgins (1806–85) known as the 'lay-Bishop of the Diocese' for his involvement with church affairs.

13. Georgian Rectory: Sandy Rectory, built about 1740 and demolished in about 1960. The finest George II rectory in the county, it was the home of the county's longest serving incumbent, the Rev John Richardson, Rector from 1858 to 1913.

14. Victorian Rectory: Blunham Rectory and Parish Church photographed in about 1900 from the Glebe Field across the Ivel. The house was designed by the Bedford architect John Usher (1822–1904). a native of Blunham, for the Rev Thomas Marlborough Berry in 1874.

15. *Village Inn: The 'White Horse' at Eaton Socon in about 1895 under the proprietorship of E. Stephenson. The age of prosperity for the coaching inns was about to return with the motor car, but here 'Good Stabling' is still as important as 'Home Brewed Ales'.*

16. *The Post Office: Upper Dean Post Office and the Postmistress, Mrs Dunmore, photographed in about 1908.*

17. The Squire: Mr Wade-Gery of Bushmead Priory, Eaton Socon with his groom and pony. Photograph taken about 1900.

18. The Gamekeeper: W. Brewer, the Tingrith keeper, about 1860. He is in his working clothes with leggings and stick.

19. The Rector: Dr Mountain of Blunham. Photographed in 1862.

20. The Verger: William Clarkem of Blunham Parish, standing at the church entrance with his keys of office, about 1900.

21. The School: The new school and headmaster's house at Husborne Crawley shortly after its opening in 1867. Husborne Crawley like its neighbour Ridgmont was a ducal estate village, one of several developed by the 7th, 9th and 11th Dukes of Bedford between 1850 and 1914. The standards of design, as in this compact group were high and the model villages of the 1900s included the earliest arts and crafts features in the county.

22. Lidlington School Pupils, photographed in about 1896. The pinafores for the girls were the nearest approach to school uniform.

23. Pupils of Westoning School in about 1910. Digging formed part of the regular curriculum of council schools until the Second World War.

24. The Policeman: Police Constable Butterworth of the Biggleswade Constabulary. About 1870.

25. *Village Fair: The 'statty' fair at Steppingley in about 1900. The steam round-about is set up in the forecourt of the 'French Horn' and the ironstone church of St Leonard by Henry Clutton, 1860, is in the background.*

26. *Rector's Recreation: The Rev W. H. Jackson of Stagsden, extreme right, with his gamekeeper, head gardener and general factotum, photographed in the late 1880s.*

27. Bolnhurst. Mrs Whitmore making lace outside the door of her home, Turnpike Cottage, in about 1900.

28. Gravenhurst. A village family photographed by Miss M. Collisson in their cottage garden about 1910.

29. Barton. Cottage interior about 1900. The couple are sitting in front of a range with their tea, including a ham laid out on a cricket table. Furnishings are simple but include a country-made long case clock, a Windsor chair and Staffordshire chimney ornaments.

30. Bolnhurst villagers of about 1900. From left to right, George Carroll, Samuel Newell, John Elliott and William Okins. John Elliott was the village clock-mender.

31. Parishioner in an unidentified Bedfordshire church, about 1895. One of an important series of country photographs by the virtuoso Victorian photographer Frederick H. Thurston, FRPS of Luton.

32. Elstow. William Southern, village postman and bootmaker, delivering mail to a cottage, since demolished, that stood opposite the now demolished Bunyan's cottage on the Bedford road. Bunyan's well can be seen in the background. About 1900.

33. Village Well: The Boiling Well at Millbrook with its brick hood. It was filled in by the County Council in the 1960s. Photographed about 1930.

34. Village Pump: Steppingley pump the main source of water supply for a century, it was taken down after 1964.

The Trades

35. The Village Tailor: Arthur J. Willison of Hockliffe squatting over his work at the window of his cottage on Watling Street. Willison also 'did a little in horses' and was a well-known local character. He has been immortalised as 'Mr Puddephat' in Arnold Bennett's Teresa of Watling Street *1904. Photographed about 1945.*

36. The Cobbler: Mr Stanniforth's shop at Ampthill, a watercolour sketch by Sir Albert Richardson, signed and dated 1940.

37. The Baker: Miss Jenny Newell, the Milton Ernest bakeress with a hand-cart of fresh loaves about 1920.

38. The Wheelwright: Mr Kendall's wheelwright's yard at Wilstead in about 1908. This trade sometimes ran with that of coach builder, the staple orders were farm carts costing £7 each.

39. Straw-plaiter at Barton. The stand-by craft of the cottager in the south as lace was in the north. About 1900.

40. Carrier: Mr Gaylor, the Ampthill carrier with the horse bought for him by local subscription 1920.

41. Mounted Postman: Mr Giles of Everton photographed in 1906. The mail came to the village by horse-drawn mail cart and was then delivered to the outlying estates and farms by Giles.

42. Water-cart man: Taking on water at Streatley in about 1900. Piped water in all but towns was a thing of the future till well into the present century.

43. Blacksmith: The Forge at Kempston from a photograph before 1899.

44. Woodcutters: Felling trees on the Firs at Ampthill about 1916 for the war effort.

45. Basket-makers: Thomas Smith (1820–1913), second from left, with a group of his osier peelers in about 1890. Smith, who only had half a day's schooling in his life, was the founder of the Pavenham basket industry.

46. Travelling saw-sharpener: Itinerant odd-job men were a common sight in villages, this one offered to 'make the old 'un cut like a new 'un' for 6d or 1s according to the size of the saw. Other itinerants were chair-menders, knife-grinders and sweeps. His penny-farthing is in the background.

47. Windmill: Sharnbrook's eighteenth century mill in decay showing its magnificent wooden upper structure.

48. The donkey wheel at Grange Farm, Kensworth, dated 1688. It was dismantled before the war and re-erected in the grounds of the Luton Museum at Wardown Park.

49. Odell Castle. Home of the Alston family from the early seventeenth century. The house was severely damaged by fire on 24 February 1931 when in the occupation of Rowland Crewe Alston. It was later demolished and rebuilt by the present Lord Luke. Photograph taken about 1860.

50. Ickwell Bury. The William and Mary home of the Harvey family from the end of the seventeenth century. It was destroyed by fire in 1937 and rebuilt by A. G. S. Butler in 1938–40. The original stables and dovecote survive.

51. Melchbourne Park. The Oakley Hunt meet in front of the 1741 façade of the house in about 1910. It was the home of the St John family from 1610 and is still in the possession of their descendants.

52. Woburn Abbey. The old east front with Henry Holland's cupola and port-cochère, demolished in 1950 by order of the 12th Duke of Bedford. The range contained the ducal study, waiting rooms and a private museum.

53. Pavenham Bury. An early eighteenth century house Jacobethanised by the Franklyn family in the 1880s. Demolished in the 1950s.

54. Cranfield Court. A High Victorian mansion of 1862–64 by the Nottingham architect Thomas Hine. He was a pupil of Mathew Habershon and one can see why with the mansards, turret and stone dressings. It was for the Rev G. G. Harter, 'squarson' of Cranfield and the first house in England with double glazing. Demolished in the 1950s.

55. Chicksands Priory. Gothick mystery in James Wyatt's re-modelled dining-room of 1813 for Sir George Osborn, Bt. This photograph was taken in 1893 in the time of Sir Algernon Osborn who later sold the house and estate.

56. Wrest Park. Rococo and chintz in the Boudoir of the house Earl de Grey designed for himself between 1834 and 1839. The photograph dates from 1895, during the occupation of Earl Cowper. The house and estate were sold in 1917 to 1920.

57. The Household: Sir Anthony Wingfield of Ampthill House (seated on the right) with his sons and the Earl of Munster, on the occasion of the latter's visit in 1907. There were eighteen inside staff, reigned over by Cooper, (top right) the butler who afterwards wrote his memoirs.

58. The Guests: A house-party at Ampthill House during the visit of the Earl of Munster in 1907.

59. Informal Group: Lord Tavistock, Lady Galloway and Mrs Lowther playing cards in the Library at Woburn Abbey in January 1882.

60. Herbrand, Duke of Bedford (right) with the young Marquess of Tavistock, later 12th Duke, in the state apartments at Woburn about 1900.

61. Indian visitors at Woburn Abbey with Adeline, wife of the 10th Duke of Bedford. About 1880.

62. The staff at Bushmead Priory in about 1895. From left to right, the coachman, the cook, children of Mr Wade-Gery, the parlour maid, kitchen maid and gardener.

63. Visiting valets and ladies' maids in the grounds of Ampthill House, about 1905.

64. Charles Steel, coachman to George James Gribble, Esq, JP of Henlow Grange. About 1897.

65. The Gardeners: Head gardener and under gardeners photographed at the kitchen garden door of Wrest Park in about 1910.

66. The Gardens: Edwardian opulence in terms of shrub, lawn and gravel. The Swiss Garden at Old Warden Park, 1905.

67. Estate Fire Service: The Wrest Park Fire Brigade with their appliance, photographed in 1910. The larger country houses were self-contained communities. The engine is now in the Shuttleworth Collection at Old Warden.

68. Chauffeur and car: The Hon Whitelaw Reid's 1910 chain-driven landaulette in the stable yard at Wrest Park. It is possibly a 16–20 hp Panhard. Mr Reid was United States Ambassador from 1905 to 1912 and rented the Wrest estate.

69. *Mary du Caurroy, daughter of the Ven Archdeacon Tribe, who married in 1888, the 11th Duke of Bedford. Better known as the 'Flying Duchess', she was the first non-aristocrat to rule at Woburn for generations. A keen botanist, ornithologist and horse woman, she was involved in nursing and social work and awarded the DBE in 1928.*

70. John Burgon, Dean of Chichester. (1813–88). He was the first Bedfordshire etymologist.

71. Sir Albert Richardson (1880–1964) dressed in Regency costume, about 1920. Architect, artist and writer of Ampthill. President of the Royal Academy 1954–56.

72. Arnold Bennett (1867–1931). Novelist. Lived at Hockliffe from 1900–02 and wrote about the county.

73. The Tenant Farms: The twenty-nine staff of George Preston, tenant farmer to the Duke of Bedford on the Beckerings Park Farm at Steppingley in 1900.

74. A group of haymakers posing for the photographer in a field at Eversholt, about 1900.

75. A tranquil country scene near Caddington in July 1892. A cart-horse stands motionless in the field with sheep grazing beyond, an unspoilt landscape that was to vanish in a generation.

76. Men double digging a field at Beckerings Park Farm in 1900. The man on the right is quite evidently only there for the photograph.

77. Haymakers' lunchtime or 'baver-time' according to Bedfordshire parlance, on Gabriel Smith's farm at Eyeworth in 1904.

78. A group of corn threshers with their threshing machine at Flitton in about 1900.

79. The Luton to Bedford road near Streatley, before dipping through the Barton cutting. A recognisable part of the now busy A6 as it was in May 1895.

80. A typical view of Bedfordshire in the 1900s. A rough tree-shaded road near Stevington with a cottager drawing water.

81. Haymaking at Millbrook in the 1890s. The chapel to the right still stands, but today the whole hillside is covered with pine woods.

82. A farm labourer of 1910 holding up a mangel-wurzel that has grown through a horseshoe.

83. A small holding of 1910 somewhere in the centre of the county.

84. The south end of Streatley village photographed in 1887.

85. A family outing in a break for a farmer and his daughters at Eversholt in the early 1900s.

86. Bromham bridge photographed in about 1900.

87. Sutton pack horse bridge. The only photograph in the collection for which photographic details exist. It was taken on 18 May 1898 at 1.30 pm with an Edwards 'Special Landscape plate'. The exposure time was 2 secs at f22 using Beck's RR Lens. It was developed with Pyro-Ammonia and printed by gas.

88. Turvey bridge with the figure of Jonah, about 1900.

Townscape

89. Town Inn: The 'Peacock', Lake Street, Leighton Buzzard, one of the county's smallest pubs dating from the fifteenth century. About 1920.

90. Market Day: Leighton Buzzard's horse and cattle market held on a Whit Tuesday in about 1900. Pens for sheep surround the fifteenth century market cross, further down the hill can be seen loose knots of horses offered for sale.

91. The Green: Toddington in 1910, empty of traffic except for a distantly trundling wagon and an attentive blacksmith at his forge on the left.

92. Town Group: The Shambles at Potton c.1930, a charming countrified omnium gatherum *rather French in feeling. It was too much of a temptation for tidy minded councils and was cropped of its real distinction in the mid-1950s.*

93. Town Centre: The Market Place at Ampthill in August 1900. The Ossory pump still retains its lantern, the corner shop its gothic window and the 1840 house on the right is still the Post Office. All these were altered or moved by 1914. Horse dung in the street awaits an eager householder.

94. Town Delivery: A light delivery cart waits in Bedford Street, Ampthill in about 1860. Opposite is the pedimented door and red brick façade of Brewery House now demolished and a giant elm stands on the site of the Fire Station, now the Council offices.

95. *Segenhoe church near Ridgmont, thirteenth and fourteenth century with Georgian additions but abandoned after 1855 for Sir G. G. Scott's Germanic All Saints. About 1900.*

96. *Old St Margaret's, Lidlington, Abandoned after 1886 and demolished before 1965. One of the finest sites for a church in the county.*

97. All Saints, Chalgrave. One of the finest of the county's parish churches with an untouched thirteenth to fourteenth century interior. The photograph shows the result of the tower collapse of 1889. The upper tower was never rebuilt.

98. St Mary, Woburn, 1865–68 by Henry Clutton. Perhaps the finest Victorian church in the county and built for the 8th Duke of Bedford. This photograph shows the magnificent East window by Kempe and the reredos by Caroe. About 1900.

99. Wesleyan chapel at Wilstead, built in 1841. There was a good deal of non-conformist building in the villages in the second half of the century, classicism giving way to gothic. Photograph about 1900.

100. The Quaker Meeting at Ampthill in about 1920. Simple eighteenth century furnishings, joined stools and a tortoise stove in a sectarian setting last used in 1900.

Transport

101. Grocer's van: An immaculate turn out of Matthews' Stores van of Biggleswade, dealers in 'Groceries, Provisions, Wines & Spirits, Beers &c'. About 1900.

102. Spring cart: Loading up with market produce at Flitton in 1900.

103. Carrier's cart: The Wilstead carrier with his family in the yard of the 'Woolpack' public house, about 1910.

104. Bicycle: The Rev Harry Pollard, Vicar of Millbrook with a boneshaker. About 1920. This form of cycling was long a thing of the past at this date.

105. Ralli car: The lady whip is Miss Newman of Ampthill and the pony 'Fidget'. Photograph taken about 1910 at her home the former 'Red Lion' public house.

106. Horse bus: A two-horse bus at the 'Sugar Loaf' at Leagrave in about 1900. The local bus looks as if it may have been hired for a wedding party.

107. Closed landau: The High Sheriff's carriage in front of Bromham House during the Shrievalty of W. H. Allen, JP 1904–05. Mr Allen and his chaplain, the Rev C. W. Browning of Bromham are about to enter the coach. Bromham House, now part of the Bromham Hospital was designed in 1897 by the architect G. P. Allen in the Tudor style. It had a Norman & Beard organ in the tower.

108. Break: Driving in the Steppingley woods about 1900.

109. Motor bus: A 1912 vehicle on the Bedford to Newport Pagnell run outside the 'Three Cranes' public house, Turvey. The photograph may date from 1919 when the National Omnibus Company began operating.

110. Charabanc: A party of happy Bedfordians off to visit the Wembley Exhibition of 1924.

111. Sharnbrook Station. Originally part of the Hitchin and Leicester railway, first opened to passengers in 1857 and then incorporated in the Midland Railway. It closed in 1962. This view shows a stopping train pulled by an 1892 Johnson locomotive approaching the station. Photograph taken in about 1910.

112. A London & North Western Railway steam rail motor car on the Oxford and Cambridge line in 1905. Three were built by the company's chief mechanical engineer, George Whale and used on this branch. The boiler was at the front and the chimney and safety valve exhausted through vents at the back. It was fitted with swivelling steps for the halts between Bedford and Bletchley.

113. *The Choir of Maulden Meeting (now Baptist church) photographed in the 1880s.*

114. Masons and surveyors at Elstow Abbey. A photograph taken during the alterations of 1881–82 when Samuel Whitbread spent £14,000 on restorations under the direction of the Bedford architect Thomas Jobson Jackson.

115. A volunteer group of the Bedfordshire Militia about 1860.

116. *Miss Annie Baker's Lace School at Riseley, about 1914. A revival of lace-making was instituted by the Bedfordshire Lace Education Committee in about 1906.*

117. *The Barton village band, photographed outside the rectory in about 1905.*

118. The Woburn Company of Change-Ringers; Charles Herebert seated at the extreme left, H. D. Harris standing second from left between Cyril and Ernest Herbert. Founded by Charles Herbert in 1867. Photograph about 1910.

119. Cycling Club at Sandy in the 1890s. The man at the back is on a penny-farthing or more correctly, ordinary bicycle. Sandy, on the Great North Road was a 'Mecca' for cyclists and F. W. Bidlake has his memorial there.

120. Meet of the Oakley Hunt at Houghton Regis in about 1910.

121. Ampthill Town Football Club with their cup, photographed in the goal mouth in Ampthill Park during the 1910 season.

122. Aristocratic wedding: The marriage of the Hon Edith Laura St John, fifth daughter of the 16th Lord St John to Mr George Lawson-Johnston, afterwards Lord Luke of Pavenham, on 4 December 1902 at Melchbourne Park.

123. Country wedding: An unidentified group in the Maulden area after a wedding in about 1910.

124. *Bible class at Blunham in about 1910.*

125. *Archaeological Society meeting at Houghton ruins in about 1919.*

126. *Stevington: Laying a foundation stone in about 1890.*

127. *Felmersham: The annual ram sale at Felmersham Grange, the residence of Mr Henry Hilton Green, photographed in 1906.*

128. Carlton: Carlton housewives preparing to celebrate Queen Victoria's Diamond Jubilee of 1897. They are holding large joints of meat about to be cooked in the bakehouse oven.

129. Clophill: A church parade passing Ivy House on its route through the village, 13 July 1913. Some of the county's earliest scouts can be seen in the right foreground.

130. Ampthill: HRH The Princess Beatrice, youngest child of Queen Victoria, unveiling the Ampthill War Memorial on 17 May, 1921.

131. Ampthill: Her Majesty Queen Mary leaving Avenue House after a private visit to Professor afterwards Sir Albert Richardson on 28 May 1934.

132. *An early motor car accident on the Watling Street near Hockliffe in about 1905.*

133. *Dan Albone (1860–1906) of Biggleswade, inventor of the Ivel racing bicycle, at the wheel of another invention, the first British farm motor-tractor in 1902.*

134. A. E. Grimmer of Ampthill (centre) with his assistants Joe Thompson (left) and Jim Brooks (right) in a field at Flitwick in about 1913–14. The Bleriot monoplane was a 1909 model bought by Mr Grimmer in 1912 and flown until the outbreak of war. It is now in the Shuttleworth Collection at Old Warden and is the only one of its type still airworthy.

135. Mary, Duchess of Bedford, the 'Flying Duchess' standing in front of her plane on the landing strip at Woburn in about 1934. She was lost over the North Sea in 1937.

136.[1] *Bedford Royal Engineers Volunteers straddling a pontoon bridge over the Ouse. Photographed in about 1914.*

137. The main ward of the temporary military hospital which was established by Mary, Duchess of Bedford in Henry Holland's Riding School at Woburn between 1915 and 1918.

138. Road mending team of Bedfordshire County Council, photographed on the main Bedford to Northampton Road at Bromham near 'Salem Thrift', about 1910.

139. The foundry of H. P. Saunderson's agricultural machinery works at Elstow in about 1906. The man in the centre is in charge of the moulding boxes for small parts.

140. Woburn Cottage Hospital by the architects Adams and Holden, founded by Mary, Duchess of Bedford in about 1910 and now the Maryland Adult Education College.

141. The interior of the first airship hangar at the Royal Airship Works, Cardington, built in 1917 and extended in 1927. For some years it was the largest structure in the British Empire. The women employees are working on the skin of an airship.

142. The airship R38 leaving her shed at Cardington for trials in June 1921. The mounting of the engines can be clearly seen as well as the trap door in the bow and the balanced elevators and rudders.

143. The airship R101 moored at the mast at Cardington in about 1930. It was hoped that this airship would open up a new route between Britain and India but it crashed near Beauvais on its first flight out, killing forty-eight of the passengers.

144. *Canal landscape in the west of the county. The Grand Junction Canal at Leighton Buzzard, photographed about 1905.*

145. *Tempsford Hall near Sandy, during the time of William Stuart (1798–1874) MP for Bedford borough. From an early nineteenth century watercolour.*

ACKNOWLEDGEMENTS

During the preparation of this book I have had invaluable advice from Miss Patricia Bell, BA, the County Archivist; Mr Frank Hackett, FGS, AMA, Curator of the Luton Museum; Miss Halina Grubert, Curator of the Cecil Higgins Art Gallery; Mr Roger Thompson, of Bedford Borough Library and Mr Henry Joyce, Curator of Woburn Abbey. I have benefited from Mr Alan Cirket's unrivalled knowledge of the county and Mr F. G. Cockman's detailed study of its railways. Last but not least, I am grateful to Mr Harold White for asking me to do the book and for allowing me to use blocks from *The Bedfordshire Magazine*.

I am grateful to the following who have lent me photographs. The Marquess of Tavistock, The Hon Hugh Lawson-Johnston, Mr T. Bagshawe, Mrs H. Brooker, Miss M. Collison, Mrs Eileen Davies, Mr John Lowe, Mr Charles Mathews, Mr Harry Newman, Mrs M. J. Robinson, Mr Andrew Underwood, Mr Richard Wildman and Miss E. G. Whitmore. Miss A. Buck kindly assisted in dating costumes.

SOURCES OF PHOTOGRAPHS

Public

County Record Office 7, 8, 9, 10, 15, 17, 18, 19, 20, 22, 24, 25, 38, 42, 43, 62, 64, 66, 73, 74, 76, 78, 80, 85, 86, 88, 90, 91, 99, 101, 102, 109, 114, 115, 119, 124, 125, 126, 127, 137, 145.

Bedford Borough Library 1, 13, 21, 47, 53, 87, 89.

Luton Museum 29, 31, 33, 39, 48, 52, 75, 79, 84, 93, 95, 120, 128, 133, 134.

Private

The Marquess of Tavistock 59, 60, 61, 69, 135.

The Hon Hugh Lawson-Johnston 4, 51, 116, 122.

Author 3, 36, 40, 44, 55, 56, 58, 63, 71, 92, 94, 100, 104, 121, 130, 131.

Mr T. Bagshawe 35, 46, 110.

Mrs H. Brooker 41.

Miss M. Collisson 28, 117.

Mrs Eileen Davies 103.

Mr John Lowe 23, 98, 140, 144.

Mr Charles Mathews 57.

Mr Harry Newman 2, 5, 11, 12, 26, 49, 50, 107, 111, 112, 132, 136, 138, 139, 141, 142, 143.

Mrs M. J. Robinson 37.

Mr Andrew Underwood 6, 34, 65, 67, 68, 81, 82, 83, 96, 105, 108, 113, 123, 129.

Mr Richard Wildman 14, 54.

Miss E. G. Whitmore 27, 30.